Royal Review

The Royal Year photographed by Tim Graham

Royce
PUBLICATIONS

Introduction
by Tim Graham

In a year in which the Royal Family's travels took me to India, Kenya, Bangladesh, The Gambia, Upper Volta, Jersey, Guernsey, Sark, Norway, Germany, France, Liechtenstein, America, and Jordan there was certainly no shortage of material for me to choose from to complete this *Royal Review*.

This year not only did the Royal Tours offer the opportunity for some marvellous pictures – but also the State Visit by the Amir of Bahrain, the D-Day celebrations in Normandy, 'informal' photocalls with Prince William, the announcement of a second baby for the Prince and Princess of Wales, a new job for Prince Andrew on HMS *Brazen*, and much more besides.

No two years are ever the same in the life of the Royal Family. Although several traditional ceremonies are repeated every year they will often produce quite different and interesting pictures. A good example is this year's Trooping the Colour when Prince William joined his cousins Peter and Zara Phillips and the rest of the Royal Family on the balcony at Buckingham Palace. It was for him the first of many hundreds of ceremonial occasions he will witness in his lifetime. It was an historic moment that gave me some of the most informal and relaxed pictures I have ever taken at this formal event.

I hope you will like the photographs I have taken during the royal year 1983–4.

TIM GRAHAM

First published in 1984 by Park Lane Press,
40 Park Street, London W1Y 4DE

First Michael Joseph edition 1984
Michael Joseph Ltd,
44 Bedford Square, London WC1B 3DU

ISBN: 0 7181 2505 3

Copyright © Tim Graham 1984

Designer: Martin Bristow

Text set by SX Composing Ltd, Rayleigh, Essex, England
Colour originated by Gilchrist Brothers Ltd, Leeds, England
Printed and bound by Severn Valley Press Ltd, Caerphilly, Wales

Summer 1983

Prince Edward at the helm of a Flying Fifteen during the world-famous Cowes Week Regatta which takes place every year at the beginning of August. Prince Philip and other members of the Royal Family usually attend, staying on board HMY *Britannia*.

Happy 83rd Birthday to the Queen Mother

On 4 August the Queen Mother celebrated another birthday and her sixtieth as a member of the Royal Family since her marriage to the Duke of York in 1923. She was born while Queen Victoria was still on the throne and is now a great-grandmother several times over. Not only is the Queen Mother doted on and revered by her own family, she is also the nation's granny that everybody, both young and old alike, would love to have. Her celebrated smile and warmth, her bravery in moments of danger and her enthusiasm for life have made her famous throughout the world and, although in her eighties, she is still hard at work, carrying out over 150 public engagements each year.

Below: The Queen and Princess Margaret, accompanied by some of their children, generally visit the Queen Mother on her birthday at Clarence House and walk out with her to the gates to acknowledge the cheers of the crowd. *Right:* The Queen with her niece, Lady Sarah Armstrong-Jones. *Facing page:* A delighted Queen Mother greeting the well-wishers.

This page: Princess Anne and Captain Mark Phillips, who are both keen and competitive riders, organized a one-day equestrian event for the first time on 6 August at their Gloucestershire home, Gatcombe Park. *Facing page*: The Princess of Wales in a relaxed mood watching Prince Charles play polo at Cirencester on 9 August.

The Royal Family's annual holiday in Scotland

Every year in August the Queen and her family look forward to the Balmoral holiday and a much-needed break from the strenuous schedule of public engagements. The estate is set deep in the Highlands and surrounded by wild moors, mountains and miles of uninhabited deer forests. It has been royal property since 1851 when Queen Victoria and her husband fell in love with the grandeur of the Highland scenery and the bracing air. The days are filled with relaxing but energetic outdoor activities such as shooting, stalking, fishing and excursions to favourite picnic spots on the hills surrounding the castle.

Facing page: The Queen inspecting men of the Royal Scots Guards who always form the guard at Balmoral when the Royal Family is in residence. *Above*: Prince Philip wearing the Royal Family's personal tartan – the grey, red and black Balmoral Tartan – which he often wears when in Scotland. *Below*: The Queen and Princess Anne at Balmoral.

Facing page: Prince Andrew, proudly sporting a beard which was destined to last only a few weeks, with Prince Edward at Balmoral on 14 August. *Above and below left*: The annual presence of the Royal Family at the Braemar Gathering has made the event one of Scotland's great tourist attractions. *Below right*: The Queen's much-loved corgis returning to London from Balmoral.

Above left: Prince Andrew at RAF Finningley for the Battle of Britain At Home Day on 17 September. *Above right:* The Princess of Wales in Bedfordshire on 20 September. *Below:* At the end of September the Prince and Princess of Wales took Prince William to Balmoral for a relaxing weekend. *Facing page:* In October Prince Edward began his studies at Jesus College, Cambridge where he is to read Archaeology and Anthropology. He is seen here with the Master of the College, Sir Alan Cotterell and his wife.

Left: King Constantine of the Hellenes with his sister, Queen Sophia of Spain at the christening of his daughter, Princess Theodora, on 20 October. *Below:* The Queen, one of the godmothers, with Queen Anne-Marie of the Hellenes and her baby. *Facing page:* To mark the centenary of the Boys' Brigade the Queen Mother attended a service at St Paul's Cathedral on 27 October.

The unveiling of the statue of Earl Mount-batten of Burma

On 2 November the Royal Family gathered at Whitehall in London to watch the Queen unveil the statue of Earl Mountbatten of Burma who had been assassinated by Irish terrorists in 1979. A much-loved member of the Royal Family, Lord Mountbatten had been at the forefront of some of the most crucial moments of twentieth-century British history, as well as being a distinguished war leader and the last Viceroy of India.

Right: The statue of Earl Mountbatten of Burma. *Below left*: The Princess of Wales with Prince Andrew and Princess Margaret. *Below right*: Princess Anne and Prince Edward, seen for the first time in public in his uniform of the Royal Marines. *Facing page above left*: Prince and Princess Michael of Kent. *Above right*: Prince Andrew and Princess Margaret. *Below from left to right*: The Duke and Duchess of Gloucester, Princess Alice Duchess of Gloucester, Princess Anne, Prince Edward, Prince Andrew, Princess Margaret, the Princess and the Prince of Wales, King Olaf of Norway and the Queen Mother. *Overleaf:* The Queen unveiling the statue with the Prime Minister, Mrs Thatcher, and the Earl's elder daughter, Countess Mountbatten.

The Queen and Prince Philip's Tour of Kenya, Bangladesh and India

In an increasingly divided world, the Queen places great value on the links that bind together the Commonwealth countries and takes her duties as Head very seriously. She tries to visit the member countries regularly and in November she and Prince Philip paid State Visits to Kenya, Bangladesh, which she was visiting for the first time, and India which was hosting the biannual Commonwealth Heads of Government meeting. The visit to Kenya had a special significance as the Queen and Prince Philip revisited Treetops where they had been staying at the moment of the Queen's accession on the death of her father, George VI, in February 1952.

Right: The Queen with President Moi of Kenya on the reviewing stand at Nairobi Airport. *Below*: The Queen inspecting the Guard of Honour at the airport, escorted by General Sawe. *Facing page*: The Queen walking to the Parliament Buildings in Nairobi.

The Queen and Prince Philip at the Remembrance Day Ceremony at the Commonwealth War Graves Commission Cemetery in Nairobi on 11 November. This was the first time in her reign that the Queen missed the ceremony at Whitehall in London.

Facing page: The Queen at the official State banquet given in her honour by President Moi. *This page:* On 12 November the Queen travelled in the Presidential train to Thika, famous for its beautiful flame trees with bright red flowers.

Facing page: Two rangers, one armed with an elephant gun, escort the Royal party through the bush to the watering hole where Treetops is situated. *Above:* When Princess Elizabeth and her husband visited the hotel in 1952 it was surrounded by forest full of big game but since then, elephants have destroyed much of the vegetation for miles around. *Below:* The present hotel is much larger than the three-bedroomed one built into fig trees originally visited by the Princess.

Above: The Queen inspecting the guard of honour at Bangabhaban, the Presidential palace in Bangladesh. *Below:* Visiting the Save the Children Fund in Dhaka. *Facing page:* The Queen being briefed on local affairs in Bairagpur, a typical Bangladeshi village.

Above: In Bairagpur the Queen was shown a display of village crafts and a handloom demonstration. *Below*: Brightly clad women greeting the Queen and President Chowdhury with flower petals at a civic reception. *Facing page*: The Queen glittering with diamonds and pearls at the Return Banquet held at Shamolee, the British High Commissioner's Residence in Dhaka.

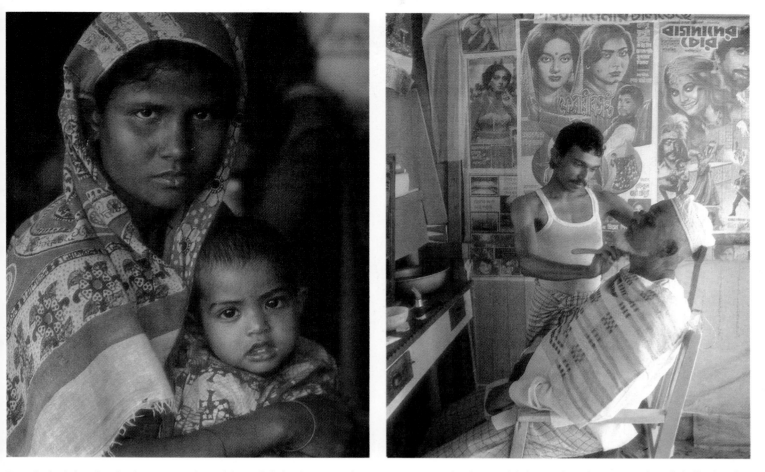

Bangladesh is a land of contrasts but although it is the second poorest country in the world, it produced a very colourful display for the Queen, including (*facing page*) an immaculately turned-out Presidential guard and (*below*) a colourful Royal train bedecked with flowers and flags which took the Queen to Sripur. *Overleaf:* The Queen leaving Bangladesh for India on 17 November.

On the first day of her visit, the Queen met Mrs Gandhi, the Prime Minister of India at the Presidential palace in New Delhi. The State Visit had been timed to coincide with the Commonwealth Heads of Government meeting, hosted this time by Mrs Gandhi.

Facing page: On the first evening of the State Visit the President gave a State Banquet at which the Queen wore her Russian tiara and magnificent sapphires. *Above*: On the following morning she paid a visit to the Red Fort in Old Delhi, famous for its red sandstone walls. *Below*: The Queen then visited St Thomas's School for girls, the last remaining Anglican school in Delhi.

At the school, senior girls dressed in male costume 'carried' the Queen in a 'palki', an eighteenth-century embroidered sedan chair with no seat originally used by noble ladies and brides. The Queen seemed to enjoy every minute of her walk!

Above: The Queen viewing Golconda Fort from the Qutab Shahi tombs in Hyderabad, an ancient Muslim city with many old and sacred monuments. *Below:* A local theatre group at the Qutab Shahi tombs. *Facing page:* Being presented with flowers.

Facing page: Hyderabadi girls dressed up in their spectacular costumes for the Royal visit. *This page:* The Queen at Devara Yamzal, a village near Hyderabad where she paid a visit to the temple. Outside the temple she was greeted by local musicians. During her tour she was escorted by village women dressed in beautiful saris.

This page: In Devara Yamzal the Queen was shown an exhibition of handicrafts and watched a display of dancing. *Facing page:* In a temperature of 100°F the Queen visited the National Defence Academy at Pune, where India's army officers are trained.

Winter 1983-4

Prince William's first public walkabout at Kensington Palace

On a cold grey morning shortly before Christmas, the Prince and Princess of Wales invited the world's press to record Prince William's first public walkabout in a small, private walled garden at their London home, Kensington Palace. The eighteen-month-old prince, dressed warmly in a navy-blue quilted suit, was at first startled by the noise of the clicking cameras and tried to escape through the garden gate no less than three times. Then, encouraged by his parents, he walked up and down in front of the photographers with a serious expression on his face. He also showed the press that he had mastered the art of the royal wave!

The Malcolm Sargent
Cancer Fund for Children

Facing page: The Princess of Wales in Manchester to attend a concert shortly before Christmas. *This page:* In January the Prince and Princess of Wales took a short skiing holiday in Liechtenstein posing for photographers on the first afternoon.

Facing page: The Princess of Wales at the Ritz Hotel in London to unveil a portrait of her husband. *This page:* Later in February she made her first solo trip overseas to Norway to watch the première of the London City Ballet's production of *Carmen*. The next morning she visited the British Embassy to meet members of the local British community.

Princess Anne's African Safari

On 16 February Princess Anne began a gruelling ten-day tour of Africa as President of Save the Children Fund. She visited Morocco, The Gambia and inland Upper Volta where one child in two dies within six months of being born – either from starvation or disease. She undertook arduous journeys travelling for many hours along rutted dirt tracks in a Land Rover. She was accompanied by Fund workers throughout her tour and visited many more Save the Children Fund doctors, nurses and volunteers while meeting the families who live in the drought-stricken regions. At all times she showed her concern for the children and did much as a 'working' President to raise morale.

Right: The Princess arrived in Banjul in The Gambia for the Independence anniversary celebrations. *Below:* On 17 February after a drive through the crowded streets of Banjul the Princess was received by the President, Sir Dawda Jawara at the State House. She was presented with the gold key to the capital by the mayor and given three kaftans.

Above: Earlier in the day Princess Anne visited the Medical Research Council Laboratories. *Below:* She toured both the Out Patients' Clinic and the laboratories.

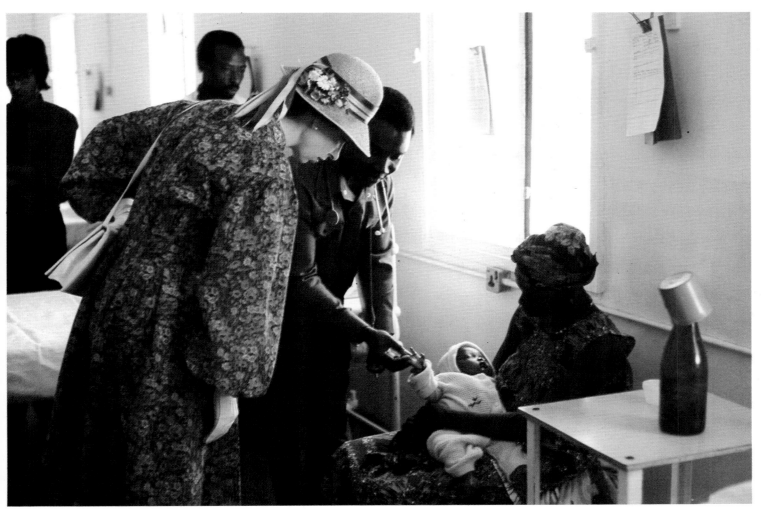

Facing page: Saturday, 18 February, was The Gambia's Independence Day. Princess Anne watched the parade and ceremony with the President. *This page:* The previous evening she attended a reception at the State House. She is accompanied by the President, his second wife Lady N'Jaimeh, and government officials.

The next part of Princess Anne's safari took her up-country into the heart of The Gambia. Here she visited mud-hut villages and inspected the often difficult living conditions that the people endure.

Above: Later that day, 19 February, the Princess helped operate the rope ferries across the river to Georgetown. *Below:* On 20 February she visited Bansang Hospital where Chinese doctors work closely with Save the Children Fund volunteers to help care for the people suffering from famine, disease and poverty.

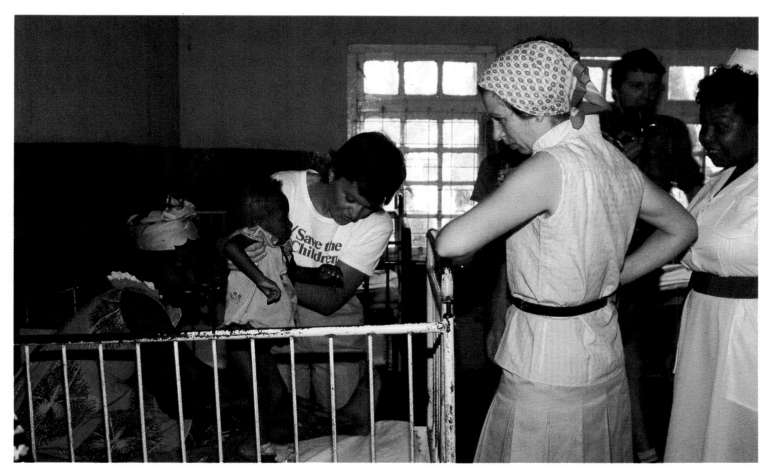

Accompanied by Fund workers Princess Anne left The Gambia and visited the desert areas of Upper Volta where temperatures reached over 100°F. Here she visited villages and toured schools.

A visit to isolated Sebba and its hospital on 23 February meant an early start at 7.15 a.m. There was a five-hour journey back to the desert airstrip at Gorom Gorom for the return flight to Ouagadougou.

Above left: An informal Princess of Wales – bound for Balmoral during a blizzard. *Above right:* A debonair male style for a visit to Lisson Grove Health Centre in London. *Below left:* An Edwardian-style hat for a tour of a Sue Ryder Home. *Below right:* A cobalt blue outfit with a straight skirt and long jacket for a trip to Sheffield.

Above: The Queen attended the Commonwealth Day Observance Service at Westminster Abbey on 12 March. *Below:* A day at Cheltenham Races for the Queen Mother on 14 March.

This page: During St Patrick's Day the Queen Mother met the officers and the families of the Irish Guards posted at Oxford Barracks, Munster. *Facing page:* The Princess of Wales wore a stunning scarlet coat trimmed with black velvet and a matching pillbox when she was welcomed by the Lord Lieutenant during a trip to Leicester on 22 March.

The State Visit to Jordan

In March the Queen embarked on one of the most perilous and controversial tours of her reign at a troublesome time in the Middle East. The four-day visit had been threatened by terrorist activity. Security was tight with King Hussein often driving his royal guests himself. But the Queen had been determined to go ahead with the tour and to fulfil a lifetime ambition to visit Jordan and at the same time to strengthen relations between the two countries. The families of King Hussein and the Queen have been friends for many years; the King's grandfather was a guest of George VI's at Balmoral and the King himself was educated at Harrow and ascended to his throne in 1952, the same year the Queen became Elizabeth II.

On 26 March the Queen and Prince Philip were welcomed to Jordan by King Hussein and Queen Noor at Marka military airport. *Facing page:* That evening King Hussein gave a State Banquet in honour of the Queen and Prince Philip at Bassam Palace, in Amman.

Armed Bedouin guards escorted the royal party wherever they went. King Hussein accompanied the Queen on a formal visit to the Martyrs' Memorial on 27 March.

During the day the Queen also enjoyed a visit to King Hussein's stables at Hunnar run by Princess Alia, the King's daughter who is seen (*below*) sitting on the Queen's left as the royal party watches a parade of Arab stallions and mares.

Left: On 28 March the royal party had a picnic at Jawan on the shores of the Dead Sea. Here the Israeli-occupied West Bank can be seen. *Above:* The evening was a more formal affair with a banquet.

Facing page: A visit to Petra, the 2,000-year-old lost city, was one of the highlights of the tour. *Above left and left:* The royal party toured the tombs, streets and caves where five hundred Bedouins still live. *Top right:* Later a guard served welcome refreshments of tea and coffee in a low tent made of goat hair. *Above:* On 30 March after bidding farewell to King Hussein and 33-year-old Queen Noor, the Queen and Prince Philip climbed aboard their aircraft for the journey home to England.

Above left: A favourite outfit for the Princess of Wales' visit to the Royal Doulton factory at Stoke-on-Trent on 5 April. *Above right and below:* Prince Edward, a Royal Marine, was present at RAF Benson at the end of a flying lesson when the Queen and Prince Philip visited The Queen's Flight of the Royal Air Force on 6 April.

The Amir of Bahrain in Britain

The Amir of Bahrain had not visited Britain for twenty years when he had been a guest at Buckingham Palace. This time during his visit in April he stayed with the Royal Family at Windsor Castle. Bahrain had been a British protectorate since 1829 until its independence in 1971 but links between the two royal families have not been broken. Head of one of the oldest royal families in the Middle East, His Highness Shaikh Isa bin Sulman Al Khalifer entertained the Queen and Prince Philip during their visit to Bahrain and the Gulf States in 1979.

On his arrival at Windsor Castle on 10 April the Amir was welcomed by the Queen and Prince Philip in the Royal Pavilion in Home Park. Diminutive in stature but resplendent in his traditional dress the Amir was then accompanied by the Prince to inspect the guard of honour formed by the Coldstream Guards. The Prince wore the Order of Ahmed the Conqueror which the Amir presented to him in Bahrain in 1979.

Above: The Queen and the Amir drove in a State landau in a carriage procession to Windsor Castle to meet other members of the Royal Family. *Left:* Princess Alexandra and the Honourable Angus Ogilvy were also in the procession – they had officially received the Amir on his arrival at Heathrow Airport, London. *Right above:* Prince Philip shows the Amir the Royal Mews at Windsor Castle. *Below:* Afterwards he took the reins and drove the Amir back to Windsor Castle.

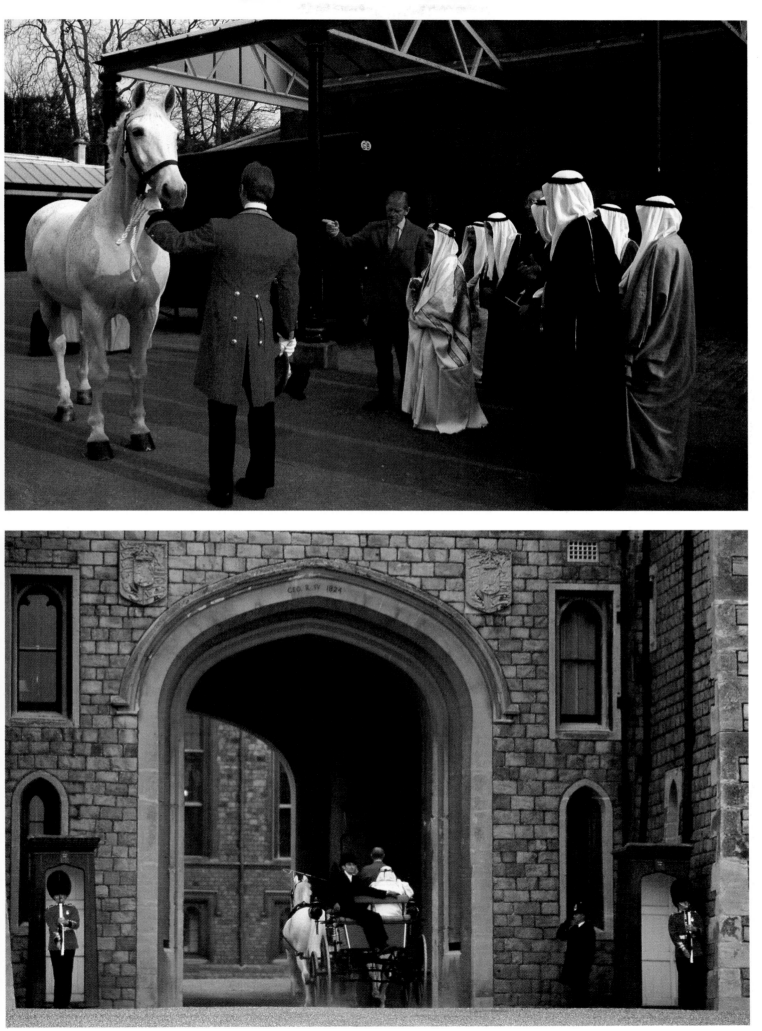

Spring 1984

The Three-Day Event at Badminton

The annual horse trials held at Badminton House heralded the beginning of spring. After the cold wintry weather of the previous weeks temperatures soared into the seventies and brought out a crowd of over 200,000 for the Cross Country event on Saturday, 14 April. The Royal Family attend the event regularly, usually staying as guests of the Duke of Beaufort but this year sadly 'the Master' of the Hunt had died a few weeks previously. The Queen stayed instead with Princess Anne and Captain Mark Phillips at Gatcombe Park.

The young Phillips children stole the show. Zara, still at a tender age, was intrigued by the Whitbread dray horses. Both she and her brother Peter mingled with the crowds to watch their father compete and then played with a friend in the afternoon sunshine.

Prince Andrew's Visit to California

Prince Andrew departed for his first official overseas tour in April. Since his return two years ago from fighting in the Falklands campaign as a Royal Navy helicopter pilot he has been the centre of much press attention and speculation – then as a hero and now as an ambassador for Britain and an eligible young prince. His trip to California caused some adverse comments but he easily charmed the crowds welcoming him with his engaging smile and handsome good looks.

Right: A rose for the Prince. *Below:* The following day actor Roy Scheider showed him the set for the space-age film 2010 which is currently being made.

Above: A Mexican lunch was held in Prince Andrew's honour in Los Angeles on 17 April. He was presented with a huge sombrero.
Below: The Prince also watched a display of Inca dancing.

Above: The Prince had a chance to display his skills as a pilot when he flew a SH60 helicopter during his visit to the U.S. Naval Air Station at San Diego. *Left:* The Prince also visited the Jet Propulsion Laboratory in Pasadena. *Facing page above left:* Prince Andrew tested an aircraft ejector seat during a tour of the McDonnel Douglas Corporation. *Above right:* At the fund-raising Royal Dinner for the British Olympic Association/U.S.A. Prince Andrew was presented with a cartoon of himself. The artist stands on the left and Tom Jones, the singer, on the right. *Right:* The Prince talks to actor, Dudley Moore.

This page: Prince Philip participating in a carriage driving event at Windsor Horse Show in May. He took up the sport ten years ago and today is ranked in the world's top ten. *Facing page:* Prince Andrew watches the action from his Range Rover.

This page: On 15 May Princess Michael of Kent attended a Spring Fair at Kensington and Chelsea Town Hall. She was presented with a sombrero and tried her luck on the tombola. *Facing page:* The previous day the Princess of Wales attended the Royal Academy of Arts annual banquet. Now in her fifth month of pregnancy she wore a demure romantic evening dress.